KATHERINE MANSFIELD

KATHERINE MANSFIELD

Jane Phillimore

Wayland

Life and Works

Jane Austen
The Brontës
Joseph Conrad
Charles Dickens
T. S. Eliot
Thomas Hardy
Hemingway
D.H. Lawrence
Katherine Mansfield
George Orwell
Shakespeare
John Steinbeck
H.G. Wells
Virginia Woolf

Cover illustration by David Armitage

First published in 1989 by
Wayland (Publishers) Ltd
61 Western Road, Hove
East Sussex BN3 1JD, England

© Copyright 1989 Wayland (Publishers) Ltd

Series adviser: Dr Cornelia Cook
Series designer: David Armitage
Series editor: Susannah Foreman

British Library Cataloguing in Publication Data
Phillimore, Jane
  Katherine Mansfield. – (Life and works)
  1. Fiction in English. New Zealand writers
  Mansfield, Katherine, 1888–1923
  I. Title II. Series
  823

ISBN 1–85210–675–1

Typeset by Rachel Gibbs, Wayland (Publishers) Ltd
Printed by G. Canale & C.S.p.A, Turin
Bound by MacLehose, Portsmouth

Contents

1

Introduction

Katherine Mansfield's short life was in many ways a tragic one. In youth she was the epitome of the 'modern' woman, bold, independent and daring, yet her reckless pursuit of freedom and adventure had terrible consequences, turning her into an invalid and eventually destroying her. She died of tuberculosis when she was only thirty-four years old, and spent the last years of her life in a desperate search for health and spiritual happiness.

She was brought up in New Zealand but as a teenager rejected both her family and the country of her birth to seek her future and fortune as an 'Artist' in London. Her spirit was restless, never content with the present time or place, and in later life she came to regard New Zealand as a lost paradise. Her childhood memories were her greatest source of literary inspiration and her best work is firmly rooted in the atmosphere of her homeland.

In character she was a mass of contradictions: brilliant, fascinating and witty, sensitive but hard and brittle, charming yet treacherous, prone to exaggeration and untruth. Virginia Woolf on their first meeting called Katherine 'cheap and hard . . . forcible and utterly unscrupulous', but later came to admire her greatly. Katherine seemed able to exercise a charm that fascinated those around her. Her friend Koteliansky summed it up: 'she could do things that I disliked intensely, exaggerate and tell untruths, yet the way she did it was so admirable, unique, that I did not trouble at all about what she spoke, it was just lovely.'

Opposite *'I am a writer first'. Katherine Mansfield at the age of 25: already a critical success with the publication of her first book,* In a German Pension.

6

Katherine Mansfield was an excellent actress and mimic and enjoyed the drama of disguise, often temporarily changing her name (even 'Katherine Mansfield' was a pseudonym: she was christened Kathleen Beauchamp) to suit a different mood or facet of her personality. She had a chameleon ability to fit in with those around her, and in letters to different friends she would assume a different mask – sometimes literary and effusive, sometimes sharp and practical, sometimes dramatic and witty. She was acquainted with many of the most famous literary figures of the day, including D.H. Lawrence (through whose novels she stalks as a dark-haired, thin-lipped, sharp-tongued young woman), Virginia Woolf, James Joyce, Bertrand Russell, Lytton Strachey and many others of the Bloomsbury group. Like them, she was questioning the accepted values of post-Victorian society and was seeking to establish a new concept and form of artistic expression.

In the history of English literature it is for her innovatory contribution to the development of the short story that Katherine Mansfield is today best remembered. But her greatest gifts were her ability to express in writing her almost spiritual enjoyment of the natural world, to create a mood and capture the essence of a swiftly passing moment, and a subtle, endearing humour. She was a natural writer, and the fluency of her style can best be appreciated from the letters and journals which flew day by day from her busy pen. In her stories she dealt with the ordinary emotions of ordinary people. The themes that occur again and again are those of loneliness, frustration and fear of death, all of which Katherine Mansfield herself experienced in no small measure during her lifetime. Her illness isolated her but at the same time made her more dependent on her husband John Middleton Murry and close friend Ida Baker; proudly and perhaps in self-protection she dedicated all her weakening energies towards perfecting her craft.

The best of Katherine Mansfield's work was written during a concentrated five year period towards the end of her life when she knew she was dying. Today, most critics agree that her illness and premature death prevented her from fulfilling her potential as a writer. As it is, her extraordinary writing talent, her fascinating personality and the tragedy of her short life make Katherine Mansfield one of the most intriguing literary figures of this century.

1922: Katherine with her second husband, editor, writer and critic, John Middleton Murry.

2 Colonial Origins

Katherine Mansfield was born Kathleen Mansfield Beauchamp on 14 October 1888. She was the third daughter and middle child of Harold and Annie Beauchamp. Her parents had married in 1884, and set up home in a modest yet comfortable house in Wellington with Annie's mother, Granny Dyer, and sister Belle.

Katherine's father, an energetic, strong-willed man, was to become extremely rich and successful as a banker and businessman and was eventually knighted for his services to the government of New Zealand. Katherine once described him as 'thoroughly commonplace and commercial' and she always resisted his attempts to turn her into a conventional, genteel young lady. Her mother Annie was beautiful, delicate, aloof and had social ambitions. She was never openly affectionate towards her children and observers have noted that she seemed to hold Katherine in dislike. Granny Dyer was a more motherly figure: she was practical, patient and kind, and looked after the Beauchamp children when their parents were away on their frequent long trips to Europe and the USA. The young Katherine and her grandmother had a very special love for each other.

In many of her New Zealand stories, Katherine drew directly from her own childhood experiences. The character of the father in the stories is often cast as a pompous and self-deluding figure. He takes himself and his position as the head of the family very seriously and, though he is always humoured by his womenfolk, he is

Opposite *The Beauchamp family in 1898. At the back, from left: Vera, Jeanne, the bespectacled 'Kathleen' and Mrs Beauchamp. At the front: Chaddie, Granny Dyer and Leslie.*

Below *Her childhood in New Zealand was the inspiration for many of Katherine's stories. Here we see her in 1898, probably in the garden at Karori, with her brother and sisters.*

mocked and excluded too. The mother and the grandmother in the stories are often contrasted – the mother languid and a little bored by her children; the grandmother kind and full of understanding. Katherine's elder sisters, Vera and Chaddie, and even Kass (one of Katherine's many nicknames) also play a part in the stories.

In 1893 the family moved to Chesney Wold, a large country house in Karori, a village four miles outside Wellington. Katherine fictionalized the move in the story 'Prelude', written over twenty years later. The Beauchamps lived in Karori for five years during which time Katherine's younger brother Leslie was born, then moved back to Tinakori Road in Wellington, the setting for another of Katherine's stories entitled 'The Garden Party'.

Opposite *Joseph and Margaret Isabella Dyer, Katherine's maternal grandparents, in 1855.*

Below *Chesney Wold, the Beauchamps' country house at Karori.*

The pupils at Miss Swainson's school, Wellington, which Katherine attended from the age of 10 to 14.

Katherine once said she was 'the odd man out of the family – the ugly duckling' and as a child she was certainly moody, difficult and intense. She was also rather plump. On one occasion, after a long absence, her mother's first words to her in greeting were: 'Well, Kathleen, I see you're as fat as ever.' Katherine had inherited her father's ambition, but her energy was devoted to making her mark as an 'Artist' – perhaps in rebellion against the middle-class attitudes she found at home. When she was ten, her parents brought back from their travels a book entitled *Elizabeth and her German Garden*, written by Harold Beauchamp's cousin, Countess Elizabeth von Arnim. According to family legend, Katherine was so impressed that she at once decided to become a writer. At school 'her pencil literally ran away with her' as one teacher put it, and early attempts at fiction were printed in the school magazine. At another school Katherine was considered 'imaginative to the point of untruth', and she always enjoyed making up stories about herself to impress her friends (a trait that continued into her adult life). She was a good though not exceptional pupil, and she could be rebellious and wilful – aged thirteen, she asked one of her teachers about 'free love', a subject which in those days not even adults would have dared mention.

As well as writing, Katherine was fond of music. In 1902 she started taking cello lessons from Thomas Trowell whose twin sons, Arnold and Garnet, were exceptionally gifted musicians. Katherine idolized the whole talented family – they were so very different from her own – and thought she was in love with Arnold, though he never reciprocated her feelings. The twins soon left New Zealand to further their musical careers in Germany, though Katherine kept in touch with Arnold by post.

When she was fourteen, Katherine and her two elder sisters were sent to finish their schooling at the all girls Queen's College in Harley Street, London. The school was an unusual one at the time because it encouraged pupils to think for themselves and develop their talents in a free and easy atmosphere. It was there that Katherine met Ida Constance Baker, nicknamed Lesley Moore or 'LM'. Ida was charmed by Katherine's liveliness and strong character and the two girls quickly became close friends. In later life when Katherine became seriously ill, it was to Ida that she often turned for support and affection.

Katherine's memories of life at Queen's College were always very clear and precise. In later years she wrote:

I was thinking yesterday of my *wasted, wasted* early girlhood. My college life, which is such a vivid and detailed memory in one way, might never have contained a book or a lecture. I lived in the girls, the professors, the big, lovely building, the leaping fires in winter and the abundant flowers in summer. The views out of the windows, all the pattern that was – weaving. Nobody saw it, I felt, as I did. My mind was just like a squirrel. I gathered and gathered and hid away, for that 'long winter' when I should rediscover all this treasure . . .

(Journal 1916)

15

Arnold Trowell, a talented cellist and Katherine's first love, though she later fell in love with his twin brother, Garnet.

Katherine was always a passionate reader. During this period she was introduced to the work of the Decadents – Oscar Wilde, Paul Verlaine, Arthur Symons, Edgar Allan Poe – as well as to Shaw and Ibsen. Katherine used to copy Oscar Wilde's witty epigrams into her notebooks, and she always wanted to appear older and more worldly-wise than she really was. The most interesting story she wrote at this time is 'About Pat', an unsentimental tale about Patrick Sheehan, the Beauchamps' Irish gardener and handyman in Karori (who also appeared in 'Prelude'). 'About Pat' was published in the school magazine, which Katherine edited. She also started work on a romantic novel called 'Juliet', full of passionate but girlish outpourings, which was never finished.

While at Queen's, Katherine took cello lessons at the London Academy of Music and seemed torn between following a musical and a literary career. When her father forbade her to become a professional musician like her hero Arnold Trowell, she wrote: ' . . . it is no earthly good warring with the inevitable – so in future I shall give *all* my time to writing.' In characteristically dramatic style, the decision to be a writer was made.

Queen's College, London, where Katherine finished her education.

After three years at Queen's College the Beauchamp girls returned to New Zealand, but once at home again Katherine found herself increasingly dissatisfied with colonial life. It was all 'The Suitable Appropriate Existence, the days full of perpetual Society functions, the hours full of clothes, discussions, the waste of life.' She had an exaggerated respect for the role of the artist and all her cultural idols were European. New Zealand seemed a backwater, and she was determined to escape. But meanwhile, she did not waste her time. She practised writing constantly – sending floods of letters to her friends in England, keeping her journal and writing new stories. She went on a trip to the interior of the North Island, and her journal entries about the Maoris and the startling New Zealand landscape give an early indication of just how good her descriptive writing would become. She was also expanding her knowledge of English and French literature, reading Browning and the Brontës, Ruskin and Meredith, Balzac, Flaubert and that master of the short story, de Maupassant.

The Beauchamp family at Las Palmas, en route for England in 1903. Katherine, standing far left beside her father, looks composed yet dreamy.

Katherine was experimenting in other areas of her life, too. She fell briefly in love with two girls – the Maori princess Maata Mahupuku and Edith Kathleen Bendall, an artist. 'She enthralls me, enslaves me,' wrote Katherine of Edith, though only three weeks later she had decided 'It was a frantically maudlin relationship and one better ended.'

In October 1907, three of Katherine's stories were published in the Australian magazine, *Native Companion*, after she told the editor that she was an obscure eighteen-year-old writer with 'a rapacious appetite for everything and principles as light as my purse'. She was paid £2 – a reasonable sum at the time. The publication of these and a few other stories including 'In a Café' convinced Katherine's parents that their daughter had genuine literary talent and that she should be allowed to live in London as she so ardently desired.

'Give me the Maori and the tourist but nothing between,' wrote Katherine about her 1907 camping trip to the North Island. Here she is photographed (standing second from left) at Te Whaiti, with some of the local Maoris.

In May 1908, just before she set off for England, Katherine made a journal entry that gives a clear indication of how she saw her future as an artist and as a woman. The qualities she most admired were 'Independence, resolve, firm purpose, and the gift of discrimination, *mental clearness*' and she concluded:

Here then is a little summary of what I need – power, wealth and freedom. It is the hopelessly insipid doctrine that love is the only thing in the world, taught, hammered into women, from generation to generation, which hampers us so cruelly. We must get rid of that bogey – and then, then comes the opportunity of happiness and freedom.

Camping at Hawkes Bay in 1907.

3 London and the Bohemian Life

London in 1908 was an exciting place for an ambitious young writer to be. There was an atmosphere of change in the air: radical ideas such as socialism, feminism, women's suffrage and Freudian psychology were endlessly discussed and were considered by many intellectuals to be the foundations upon which a new and better society could be built. Debate was lively, especially in the crop of pamphlets and magazines that had sprung up, to some of which Katherine Mansfield later contributed stories. The bustling intellectual life of the city was a perfect setting for one so dedicated to living 'Life' – the exotic, bohemian life of an artist – to the full.

Her father had made Katherine an allowance of £100 a year, enough to give her a measure of independence. She took lodgings near the Trowell family in north London and immediately fell in love with Arnold Trowell's twin brother, Garnet. Garnet was also a musician – he played the violin – but he was less talented than his brother. He was shy, dreamy and gentle, and perhaps more easily under the sway of Katherine's strong personality. Within a month of landing in England Katherine was calling Garnet 'my wonderful, splendid husband' and although under-age, they planned to get married. At first, Katherine was warmly accepted into the Trowell family, but then things started to go wrong. She fell out with Garnet's parents, perhaps because they discovered that the young couple were lovers, and was banned from the house.

Trafalgar Square, London, 1910.

Opposite *Katherine Mansfield, the budding writer, in 1906.*

Meanwhile she had met George Bowden, a singing teacher in his early thirties who apparently found her fascinating. On just a few weeks' acquaintance he proposed marriage and was accepted. They were married on 2 March 1909, with Katherine unconventionally dressed in black. Ida Baker, Katherine's close friend, was witness. As it happened, Katherine had very rapid second thoughts. She refused to consummate the marriage and left George Bowden on their wedding night.

Why did Katherine marry Bowden? Biographers disagree, but it seems likely that she discovered she was pregnant by Garnet whom, because of his parents' opposition, it was now impossible to marry. Katherine's second husband, John Middleton Murry, said later that he believed she was pregnant as early as November 1908. In those days it was a disgrace for a woman to give birth out of wedlock, and that might have been reason enough for Katherine to want to get married – to anyone – quickly.

Meanwhile, alarmed by news of the marriage, Katherine's mother arrived from New Zealand and immediately carried her daughter off to Bad Wörishofen, a health resort in Bavaria, presumably so that Katherine could have the child quietly out of scandal's way. Then, leaving Katherine alone and pregnant, Mrs Beauchamp returned to New Zealand where she showed her disapproval of her daughter's wild behaviour by cutting her out of her will.

Katherine lost her baby in Bavaria, but in one way the time she spent there was a blessing. She had written almost nothing in the ten months she had been in London: now she found herself alone and with the leisure and inclination to examine the behaviour of those around her. The witty, satirical sketches and short stories she wrote about the Germans she met were eventually published as her first book, *In a German Pension*.

While in Bavaria, Katherine stayed in the Pension Müller, a hotel where middle-class Germans – whom she saw as horribly pompous, self-satisfied and obsessed with their bodily functions – would go for a few weeks each year to take a health cure. Katherine's sharp pen pokes cruel fun at these poor souls who at the slightest opportunity would launch into complicated detail about their health:

'A beautiful day,' I cried turning to Fraulein Stiegelauer. 'Did you get up early?'

'At five o'clock I walked for ten minutes in the wet grass. Again in bed. At half past five I fell asleep and woke at seven, when I made an "overbody" washing! Again in bed. At eight o'clock I had a cold-water poultice, and at half past eight I drank a cup of mint tea. At nine I drank some malt coffee and began my "cure". Pass me the sauerkraut, please. You do not eat it?'

('Germans at Meat')

25

Opposite *It was during her stay in Bavaria that Katherine gathered material for the witty, satirical sketches that were eventually published as* In a German Pension.

There is little subtlety in the characterizations in *In a German Pension*. In broad, harsh strokes, Katherine Mansfield drew an unsympathetic picture of German people, especially German men. Many of the stories are told from the viewpoint of a first-person narrator – Katherine Mansfield herself – who is a foreigner and therefore also an outsider, and who often speaks with a very supercilious tone. This figure is quick to intrude with clever, malicious comments which have the effect of distracting the reader's attention:

'Who is he?' I said. 'And why does he sit always alone, with his back to us, too?'

'Ah!' whispered the Frau Oberregierungsrat, 'he is a Baron.'

Below *A German house party in 1911. The type of middle-class Germans Katherine so despised.*

'But, poor soul, he cannot help it,' I said. 'Surely that unfortunate fact ought not to debar him from the pleasures of intellectual intercourse.'

If it had not been for her fork I think she would have crossed herself.

('The Baron')

In Bavaria, Katherine met Floryan Sobieniowski, a
28-year-old Pole with a great love of the literature of Russia
and Poland. He was later described by John Middleton

Murry as 'charming, distinguished and completely untrustworthy', but despite this, Katherine and he fell in love and made plans to live together in Paris. Katherine is thought to have fictionalized her feelings about Sobieniowski in her story 'The Swing of the Pendulum'.

Sobieniowski probably introduced Katherine to the works of the Russian writer Chekhov, to whom she was often compared. At this time Katherine turned one of Chekhov's short stories, 'Spat khochetsia' or 'Sleepyhead', into her story 'The-Child-Who-Was-Tired', collected in *In a German Pension*. Almost thirty years after her death, she was accused of plagiarism – of stealing Chekhov's story and giving it out as her own. A bitter controversy arose, and Katherine Mansfield's posthumous reputation as a writer was seriously damaged.

In fact, when compared, the two stories *are* remarkably similar. The plot is identical, as it follows a day in the life of an overworked and exhausted young child, so tired that she eventually ends up killing a crying baby so she can get to sleep. But although Katherine certainly based 'The-Child-Who-Was-Tired' on 'Sleepyhead', it was not a direct translation. She added new characters and many of her own descriptive touches. In 1910 Chekhov was not well known in England and only a few of his works had been translated. Even so, Katherine *should* have acknowledged her debt to the Chekhov story. In later life she was always resolutely against the re-publication of *In a German Pension*. Although she claimed this was because the book was 'early, early work' and was 'not good enough', perhaps it was also because she knew it contained, in the words of one biographer, 'a small Chekhovian time bomb ticking away inside'.

In her writing Katherine Mansfield was always interested in catching the mood of a particular moment. In the *German Pension* stories her method of doing this is rather crude and immature, with weak characterization that sometimes borders on caricature. Yet two stories in the collection stand out because they prefigure the subtle, complex relationships evident in Katherine Mansfield's more mature work. The first of these is 'Frau Brechenmacher Attends a Wedding', in which a German *hausfrau*, worn out and downtrodden after years of bearing children and looking after her husband, family

Co-editors of Rhythm: *Katherine Mansfield and John Middleton Murry in 1913.*

and home, attends a wedding. This prompts her to reflect on her own joyless marriage and subjugation to her selfish, uncaring husband:

> 'Ah, every wife has her cross. Isn't that true, my dear?'
> Frau Brechenmacher saw her husband among his colleagues at the next table. He was drinking far too much, she knew – gesticulating wildly, the saliva spluttering out of his mouth as he talked.
> 'Yes,' she assented, 'that's true. Girls have a lot to learn.'
>
> ('Frau Brechenmacher Attends a Wedding')

The story is told objectively and without emotion, but in strong, vivid language and with extremely realistic use of dialogue. The reader is moved to feel both anger and pity for this long-suffering *frau* who is powerless to improve her situation – the woman's lot.

The second story, 'A Birthday', is a tale of childbirth. Although the story is ostensibly set in Germany, the descriptive passages conjure up images of New Zealand – Katherine Mansfield was already drawing upon the creative inspiration of her homeland.

The plot is a simple one: Andreas Binzer's wife is expecting her third child, and he is sent off to fetch the doctor, who returns with him and delivers his 'son and heir'. The story is told by Andreas Binzer as an interior monologue, a record of the character's thoughts as they occur, and shows the workings of his mind during this crucial time. Like most of the men in the *German Pension* stories, Binzer is selfish and self-satisfied. He is also nervous and preoccupied with his own suffering. 'I'm too sensitive for a man,' he says, 'that's what's the matter with me.' He easily manages to dismiss the terrible labour pains his wife is enduring upstairs:

While travelling in the North Island in 1907, Katherine stayed at the Rangitaiki Hotel. The heat, dust and isolation provided excellent background material for her story 'The Woman at the Store'.

At that moment, fainter than he had heard in the passage, more terrifying, Andreas heard again that wailing cry. The wind caught it up in mocking echo, blew it over the house-tops, down the street, far away from him. He flung out his arms, 'I'm so damnably helpless,' he said, and then, to the picture [of his wife], 'Perhaps it's not as bad as it sounds; perhaps it is just my sensitiveness.'

('A Birthday')

Sharp-witted, sharp-nosed Katherine Mansfield caricatured by George Banks in 1912.

'A Birthday' is technically interesting because by using the interior monologue, the story transfers the dramatic

action to within the character, so concentrating on Binzer's view of events and showing him up in all his conceit. This was a technique which Katherine used to great effect in a few of her later stories, including the short story 'Je ne parle pas français'.

Katherine Mansfield once wrote that 'the only way to live as a writer is to draw upon one's real, familiar life – to find the treasure'. Not only does she draw upon the New Zealand setting in 'A Birthday': one can also see shades of her father Harold Beauchamp in Andreas Binzer and of Granny Dyer in the gentle, caring grandmother. While in Bavaria Katherine miscarried and lost her baby, and the often bitter preoccupation of the German stories with childbirth, with women's traditional role in the family, and with the isolation of all human experience probably reflect her own preoccupations of the time.

When Katherine Mansfield returned to London she was introduced to A.R. Orage, the editor of *New Age*, a lively new magazine devoted to politics, literature and art. He decided to publish a series of her German stories starting with 'The-Child-Who-Was-Tired', 'Germans at Meat', 'The Luftbad' and 'The Baron'. Orage became an invaluable friend and critic who taught Katherine to be succinct and observant and to avoid her occasional tendency towards sentimentality. In 1921, Katherine wrote expressing her debt to him, saying: 'You taught me to write, you taught me to think, you showed me what there was to be done and what not to do.'

It was through the *New Age* that Katherine's work came to the attention of Stephen Swift, who offered her £15 to publish a collection of her stories as a book. In December 1911, *In a German Pension* was published. The book was a modest success, and critical opinion was on the whole favourable. Her writing was described as 'cleverly observant', 'original' and 'impish', though she 'dwelt a little too insistently on the grossness or coarseness'. As for herself, Katherine later said that *In a German Pension* was 'far too immature . . . it's not good enough . . . and besides that it's not what I mean: it's a lie.'

Although she always judged her work harshly, in this case Katherine Mansfield was right: these youthful stories are not among her best. But they are vividly alive and in theme, style, characterization and excellent handling of dialogue, contain the germ of all her later work.

4 The Restless Years

Soon after the publication of *In a German Pension*, Katherine Mansfield met John Middleton Murry, an Oxford undergraduate and co-editor of a quarterly literary magazine called *Rhythm*. Murry was young, handsome and quietly ambitious, and he and Katherine took to each other at once. Encouraged by Katherine, within a few months he had given up his studies at Oxford and moved into her flat as a lodger, though they soon became lovers. Their relationship was never an easy one, especially in the early years when Katherine, quick-witted, precocious and demanding, at times found Murry dull and unadventurous. In 1919, the year after they were married, she confessed to her journal: 'There is the inexplicable fact that I love my typical English husband for all the strangeness between us. I do lament that he is not warm, ardent, eager, full of quick response, careless, spendthrift of himself, vividly alive – *high-spirited* but it makes no difference to my love'. Despite frustrations and frequent short separations, they remained together throughout Katherine's life. (Murry, however, remarried three times after her death.)

Katherine Mansfield soon became assistant editor and a contributor to *Rhythm*. Her first work published in the journal was 'The Woman at the Store', a cleverly crafted story which deals indirectly with a murder. It is set amidst the heat and dust of New Zealand's backblocks, areas so isolated that the inhabitants can go for weeks without seeing a stranger. The piece is remarkable largely because

of the atmosphere that Katherine Mansfield manages to create: she conjures up a strange and savage world in which a once-pretty woman is driven by neglect, maltreatment and rage to kill her husband and conceal the crime. The heat, the wind, the dust, the harsh world of nature – Katherine drew upon the wild New Zealand landscape she observed during her teenage trip to the North Island – take on a malignant life of their own and prove the perfect breeding ground for human evil:

After meeting Katherine, Oxford academic life became unendurable to Murry, who left before graduating.

> All that day the heat was terrible. The wind blew close to the ground; it rooted among the tussock grass, slithered along the road, so that the white pumice dust swirled in our faces, settled and sifted over us and was like a dry-skin itching for growth on our bodies.

('The Woman at the Store')

Rhythm was set up by Murry as a vehicle to give expression to the avant-garde literature and art of England and France. In retrospect its artistic contributions (Picasso, Henri Gaudier-Brzeska, Augustus John) look more substantial than its literary ones, but the magazine nevertheless gave the 'Murrys' the opportunity to meet

some of the most interesting writers and artists of the day, including the novelist D.H. Lawrence, the poet Rupert Brooke and many of the Bloomsbury set. The magazine was plunged into financial disaster in 1912 when its publisher fled the country, leaving a debt which Murry could not pay. For a while it struggled on, changing its name to the *Blue Review*, but eventually was forced to close.

Mansfield and Murry's life during the next couple of years was restless and troubled. They were short of money, having pledged Katherine's allowance to pay *Rhythm*'s debts, and they moved frequently around London and the country, with brief trips to Paris where Katherine met Francis Carco, a writer friend of Murry.

Opposite
Handsome and in deadly earnest: John Middleton Murry in 1912.

Katherine's relationship with Murry was also full of uncertainty and dissatisfaction. In 1914 she wrote in her journal that he was '...far too absorbed in his own affairs ...he doesn't consider the people within his reach'. Later in the year she seemed determined to end the relationship, writing: 'What we have got each to kill – is my *you* and your *me*. That's all. Let's do it nicely and go to the funeral in the same carriage, and hold hands hard over the new grave, and smile and wish each other luck.'

Opposite *The war poet Rupert Brooke (1887–1915).*

The French novelist Francis Carco, in front of his second floor flat in the Quai aux Fleurs, which he lent to Katherine to write 'The Aloe'.

In February 1915 she decided to leave Murry and go to France for a week to stay with Francis Carco. It was a dramatic move. In August 1914 the First World War had broken out and Carco was stationed close to the front. Katherine had to bluff her way past the French Army officials to see him. The adventure is described in 'An Indiscreet Journey'. Francis Carco was also the major inspiration for the character of Raoul Duquette, the narrator of 'Je ne parle pas français', one of Katherine's best known stories, written early in 1918. The affair was short-lived and Katherine was soon back with Murry, though in the next year she often stayed at Carco's empty Paris flat to write.

Leslie Heron Beauchamp, Katherine's brother, who died during the First World War.

When war was declared, Katherine Mansfield's brother Leslie joined up and was sent to England for officer training. He and Katherine became very close and spent a great deal of time together reminiscing about New Zealand and their shared past. In October 1915, just a few weeks after he was posted to France, Leslie Beauchamp was killed – blown up by a faulty hand grenade. It was a terrible tragedy, and Katherine reacted with wild, bitter grief. She set off for the South of France where she could mourn in peace, and her letters and journal of this time express her sorrow and loss. 'On the mantelpiece in my room stands my brother's photograph. I never see anything that I like, or hear anything, without the longing that he should see and hear, too.' In her journal she wrote: 'I feel I have a duty to perform to the lovely time when we were both alive. I want to write about it, and he wanted me to.'

If Leslie's death prompted Katherine Mansfield to write about New Zealand, it was also at this time that she came to a decision to write within a different form or structure. Both these aims are clearly laid out in a journal entry of January 1916:

> . . . never has my desire [to write] been so ardent. Only the form that I would choose has changed utterly. I feel no longer concerned with the same appearance of things. The people who lived or whom I wished to bring into my stories don't interest me any more. The plots of my stories leave me perfectly cold . . . now [I] want to write recollections of my own country . . . It must be mysterious, as though floating. It must take the breath . . . I shall tell everything, even of how the laundry-basket squeaked . . . But all must be told with a sense of mystery, a radiance, an afterglow, because you [Leslie], my little sun of it, are set . . . No novels, no problem stories, nothing that is not simple, open.

In January 1916 Murry joined Katherine at Bandol in the South of France, and the next three months were what Murry called 'the happiest time of our lives together'. In February Katherine turned her attention to cutting and revising 'The Aloe', a story she had written the year before in Paris. The eventual result was 'Prelude', one of her greatest achievements and, like much of her work, based upon the experiences of her own life. When Katherine was a child, her family moved from Wellington into a large house in the country at Karori, and this event forms the outline for the story. The Burnell family in 'Prelude' are based on Katherine's own family and Kezia, the impulsive young girl at the centre of the story, is Katherine herself.

At the time, 'Prelude' was dramatically original, both in technique and content, because it dealt with ordinary, everyday events without having reference to a plot. The story portrays the uneventful daily life of the Burnell family – the self-important figure of Stanley Burnell, 'awfully simple, easily pleased and easily hurt'; his wife, Linda, beautiful and languid, absorbed in a world of her own imagining; the grandmother, wise, calm and dignified, providing a source of maternal comfort and warmth for both Linda and Kezia; and the children, flitting in and out of the story in their own secret, childlike way. There are twelve episodes: each concentrates on one member or the relationships between members of the family, and the whole is casually linked together to form a complete picture of the complex workings of family life. It is told in a dreamy, impressionistic form in which the inner consciousness of the characters comes vividly alive, yet overall the reader is left with a sense of impermanence, of life passing by, achieved by contrasting human existence with that of the more permanent world of nature, symbolized by the aloe tree. For example, when Linda reflects on her feelings for her husband whom she simultaneously loves and hates:

> There were all her feelings for him, sharp and defined, one as true as the other. And then there was this other, this hatred, just as real as the rest. She could have done her feelings up in little packets and given them to Stanley. She longed to hand him that last one, for a surprise. She could see his eyes as he opened that . . .
>
> She hugged her folded arms and began to laugh silently. How absurd life was – it was laughable, simply laughable. And why this mania of hers to keep alive at all? For it really was a mania, she thought, mocking and laughing.
>
> 'What am I guarding myself for so preciously? I shall go on having children and Stanley will go on making money and the children and the gardens will grow bigger and bigger, with whole fleets of aloes in them for me to choose from.'
>
> ('Prelude')

Opposite *The manuscript of the poem 'Sanary', written while Katherine was recuperating after Leslie's death.*

42

Samarai:

Her little hot worn lashes ... the bay
Through a stiff palissade of glittering palms
And here she ... lie in the heat of
Her dark head   the day
    resting upon her arms
          so still
So quiet ~~that~~ she did not ~~even~~ seem
To think to feel or even to dream

~~Beside the ~~~~ ...~~
             in
~~Hung by a ... from the ...~~

The shimmering blinding ... of sea
Hung from the shore and the ...
                              smelt
With ~~...~~ for ~~... ...~~ ...
... ... the sky and spun and spun
She ... see it still like she that
                    cant   he lay
And the little boat ~~lay~~ in it ... the
                                        flies

... ...
~~N... walks~~ ... ...
~~D...~~ ... dying ... flee
~~Y... ... ...~~ ... ...

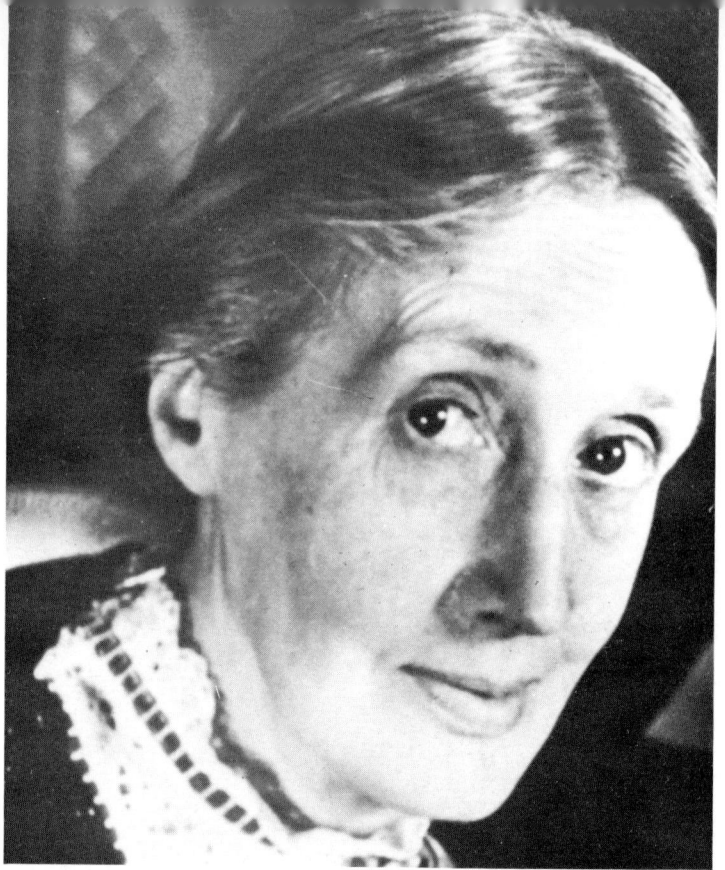

Virginia Woolf, who published 'Prelude' in 1918.

There is no climax or conclusion to 'Prelude'; Katherine Mansfield was not trying to tell a tale. Instead she was attempting to recreate life, to give an in-depth and authentic picture of the Burnell family. In a letter to a painter friend, she tried to explain her method, what she called the '*divine* bounding into the spring of things':

When you paint apples do you feel that your breasts and your knees become apples, too? Or do you think this the greatest nonsense. I don't. I am sure it is not. When I write about ducks I swear that I am a white duck with a round eye, floating on a pond fringed with yellow-blobs and taking an occasional dart at the other duck with the round eye, which floats upside down beneath me . . . In fact the whole process of becoming the duck . . . is so thrilling that I can hardly breath, only think about it. For although that is as far as most people can get, it is really only the 'prelude'. There follows the moment when you are *more* duck, *more* apple, or *more* Natasha than any of these objects could ever possibly be, and so you *create* them anew.

(Letter to the Hon. Dorothy Brett, 1917)

'Prelude' was published in 1918 by Virginia and Leonard Woolf's Hogarth Press. Katherine first met the novelist Virginia Woolf late in 1916, and had been immediately impressed by the 'trembling, glinting quality of her mind'. For her part, Virginia Woolf, always socially fastidious, was rather taken aback by Katherine Mansfield: 'In truth, I'm a little shocked by her commonness at first sight; lines so hard and cheap. However, when this diminishes, she is so intelligent and inscrutable that she repays friendship.'

The front cover of the Hogarth Press edition of 'Prelude'.

Although they never became close friends (perhaps because of some professional rivalry) the two women met and exchanged letters from time to time over the next few years. Virginia thought Katherine had 'a much better idea of writing than most' and on Katherine's death wrote in her diary: 'I was jealous of her writing. The only writing I have ever been jealous of.' Katherine, too, recognized that as writers they shared a common bond, and remarked rather gushingly in a letter to Virginia: 'We have the same job and it is really very curious and thrilling that we should both . . . be after so nearly the same thing.'

Perhaps because of her sharp, sometimes cruel wit, Katherine Mansfield found herself in great demand socially at this time with the Bloomsbury set. She flirted briefly with the painter Mark Gertler, and the philosopher and mathematician Bertrand Russell. Russell found 'her talk marvellous, much better than her writing', and literary biographer Lytton Strachey thought her 'interesting – very amusing and sufficiently mysterious . . . with a vulgarly-fanciful intellect'.

Mansfield and Murry were also very friendly with the novelist D.H. Lawrence and his wife Frieda. Lawrence is now considered a great and original writer, but at the time his passionate books outraged conventional opinion. The two couples lived near each other in 1914, and again in Cornwall in the spring of 1916.

The two or so months they spent in neighbouring cottages on Cornwall's north coast were not happy ones. Katherine thought Frieda's influence on Lawrence had changed him for the worse. She wrote humorously that Lawrence was lost 'like a little gold ring in that immense German Christmas pudding which is Frieda. And with all the appetite in the world one cannot eat one's way through Frieda to find him.' Lawrence was subject to violent bursts of rage – perhaps due in part to his tubercular condition – and he and Frieda fought endlessly. Katherine complained that they 'are both too rough for me to enjoy playing with'. Yet despite their many disagreements, Katherine Mansfield and Lawrence had an enduring affection for each other. Her influence on him was profound, and the sardonic, thin-lipped woman who features in so many of his works – for example in *Women in Love*, written while Lawrence was in Cornwall – was inspired by Katherine. (The character of Gerald Crich, also in *Women in Love*, is thought to be based on Murry.)

Opposite
Philosopher and mathematician Bertrand Russell (1872–1970), with whom Katherine is said to have had a brief flirtation.

Higher Tregarthen, Zennor, in Cornwall where the Murrys spent the spring and early summer of 1916 with the Lawrences.

In December 1917 Katherine Mansfield was diagnosed as having pleurisy and was told that if she spent another winter in England she would become consumptive. She also had a 'spot' or weakness in her lung. Her health had been deteriorating since 1910 when she had had an operation to remove a fallopian tube, probably because it was infected with gonorrhoea, a sexually transmitted disease which she had picked up in her youth. Unless treated quickly, gonorrhoea was almost impossible to control. Although it could lie dormant for years, it often spread throughout the body leaving the system seriously weakened and prone to arthritis, heart trouble and pleurisy, all of which Katherine Mansfield at some time suffered from. Resistance to other disease was also lowered. When Katherine came into contact with the then common disease of tuberculosis – perhaps from D.H. Lawrence during the months they spent together in 1914 and 1916 – she was unable to repel the infection. From that time on, she was chronically ill – and only getting worse.

Opposite *Murry, Frieda and D.H. Lawrence in 1914.*

5 'I am a writer first'

'To be alive and to be a "writer" is enough ... There is *nothing* like it!' Katherine Mansfield confided to her journal in an exuberant mood in May 1917. Ironically, this simple vision of life was to prove hard to fulfil: the rest of Katherine's life was spent battling against worsening health while trying desperately to produce the work that as a writer she knew she was capable of.

On her doctor's advice she set off to winter abroad in the South of France. Katherine loved travelling and the start of a journey was usually a great adventure, but in her precarious state of health the lengthy trip alone through war-torn France proved a nightmare. Bandol itself had changed for the worse since her visit with Murry in 1916 – nobody recognized her, it was cold, she was ill, alone and unhappy, and she was dependent on Murry's letters as on a lifeline. She wrote two stories in intense, feverish bursts: of the first, 'Je ne parle pas français', she told Murry: 'My work excites me so tremendously that I almost feel *insane* at night'. Then she dreamed the entire plot of 'Sun and Moon', a simple and rather sentimental story of childhood, and wrote it at one sitting.

'Je ne parle pas français' is an ambitious story told from the viewpoint of a cynical, self-absorbed 'little perfumed fox-terrier of a Frenchman' called Raoul Duquette. Duquette, a part-time gigolo with literary aims – he had already written three books – is sitting musing in a seedy Parisian café when, on a piece of blotting paper, he sees written the phrase 'Je ne parle pas français'. At once he remembers the tragic story of his English friend Dick Harmon and Mouse, the beautiful young girl Harmon brought to Paris and then abandoned.

Although the plot is more involved than in many Mansfield stories, the chief interest of 'Je ne parle pas français' lies in the creation and portrayal of Duquette's character. We are allowed to see the intricate inner workings of Duquette's mind: his feelings and response to life; his emotions, undisguised, often base and self-centred; his posturing, his self-preoccupation, yet also his humour, his wit, the complexity of his character. Katherine Mansfield freely ranges over events in his life – his childish encounters with a black laundry-maid, his relationship with his concierge, his 'first-rate' moment of euphoria, his consuming interest in Dick Harmon and Mouse – to give us the character of the man whole and complete. We *know* him. It is a remarkable story using what was at that time a remarkably original technique, and although we may not end up admiring Duquette, his portrayal is vibrantly alive.

'To be alive and to be a "writer" is enough . . . there is nothing like it.' *Journal*, 30 May 1917.

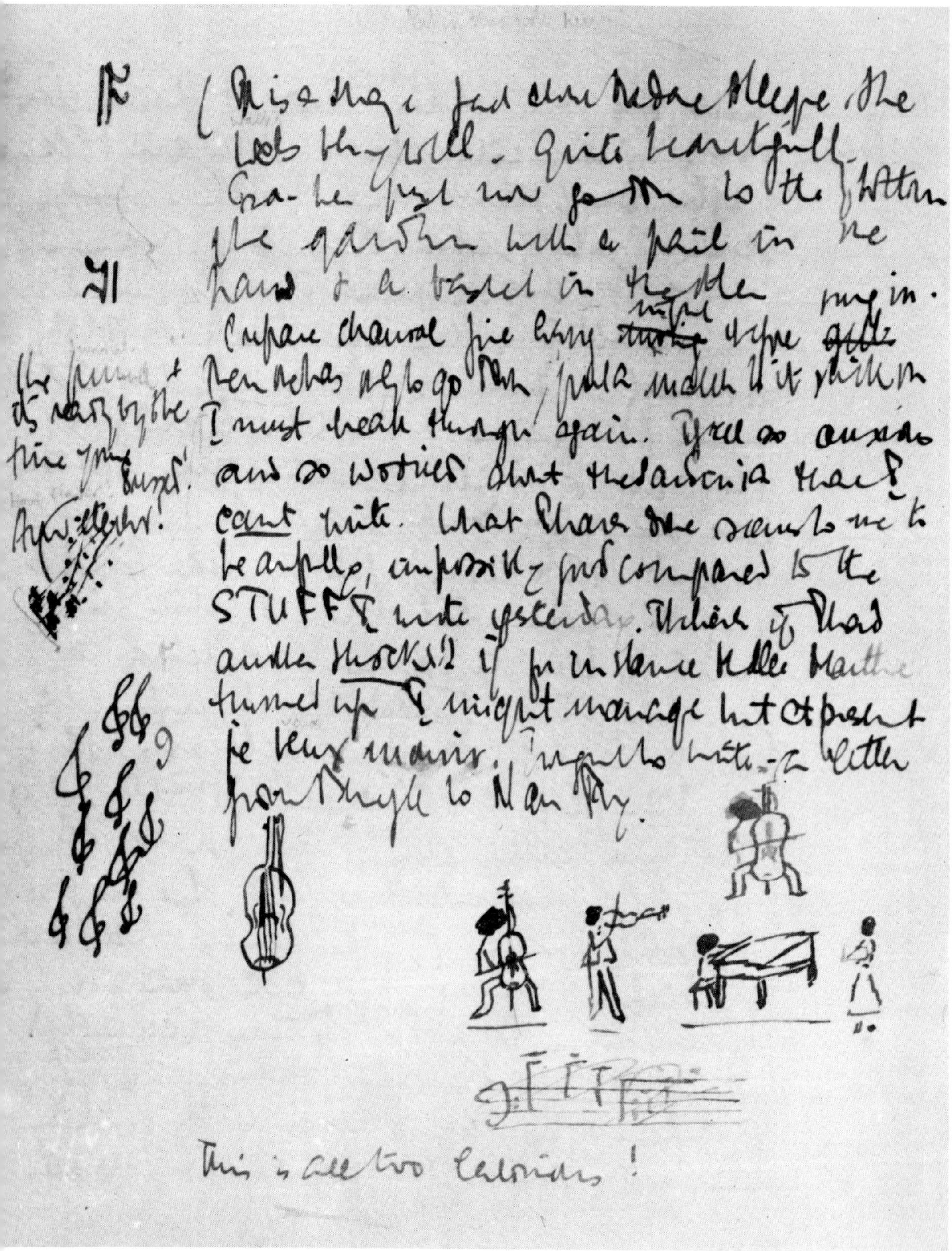

Quite beautifully.
the garden with a pail in one hand & a basket in the other singing.
I must break through again. I feel so anxious and so worried that I can't write. What I have done seems to me to be [illegible] compared to the STUFF I wrote yesterday. [illegible] if for instance Mlle Marthe turned up I might manage but at present [illegible]
This is all too [illegible]!

In February 1918, just after the unwelcome arrival of her devoted friend Ida Baker in Bandol, Katherine for the first time coughed up bright red arterial blood. In those days, before the invention of penicillin, this amounted to a death warrant – confirmation of advanced tuberculosis. From that point on, Katherine was battling with the knowledge of impending death. She lost weight and became weak, short of breath and was unable to walk without the aid of a stick. She was plunged into black depression, with violent outbursts of pure hate against Ida, against Murry, against life. Yet her illness also brought her a heightened appreciation of nature. In 1918 she wrote to Murry: 'Since this little attack I've had, a queer thing has happened. I feel that my love and longing for the external world – I mean the world of *nature* – has suddenly increased a million times . . . '

As she became more seriously ill, she wrote more poignantly about the natural world, contrasting its beauty and permanence with the often fleeting and sordid experiences of humankind.

She and Ida returned to England in the spring, though they were stranded for three terrifying weeks in Paris during the German bombardment of the city. In May 1918 Katherine's divorce from George Bowden finally came through, and she and Murry married the next day. Her marriage had provided a beacon of hope for Katherine throughout the long winter in Bandol, but almost at once she was disappointed by Murry's lacklustre response to wedded life. 'Our marriage. You cannot imagine what that was to have meant to me. And it really was only part of the nightmare, after all. You never once held me in your arms and called me your wife. In fact the whole affair was like my silly birthday. I had to keep making you remember it.'

Perhaps genuinely shocked by her frailness (she had lost over a stone during the winter) or perhaps (as Katherine sometimes uncharitably felt) worried about catching the disease himself, Murry sent Katherine off to spend a few weeks in Cornwall. There, at times, despair overwhelmed her: 'Oh God,' she wrote in an unposted letter to Murry, 'this terrifying idea that one must *die*, and may be *going* to die . . . I have suffered such AGONIES from loneliness and illness combined that I'll never be quite whole again . . . '

Opposite *Notebook scribblings while working on 'The Aloe': 'This is all too laborious!'*

53

1918: barricades at Versailles, during the German bombardment of Paris, which Katherine and Ida Baker experienced at first hand.

That autumn, Katherine and Murry moved into their first proper home together, a large, grey house in Hampstead, north London, which they nicknamed the 'Elephant'. At about the same time, Katherine saw two medical specialists who advised her to enter a sanatorium or else, one told Murry, she would have at the most only four years to live. Katherine had always refused to go into a sanatorium, partly because she thought she would not be able to abide the strict, regulated life, but also because she would not be allowed to work. Instead she spent that winter and the next summer living quietly in Hampstead with Murry.

In the New Year, Murry was made editor of the *Athenaeum*, a heavyweight weekly journal of 'Literature, Science, the Fine Arts, Music and Drama'. Katherine soon became the regular fiction reviewer, a post she held until the end of 1920. Her critical eye was lively and she took her work seriously: her reviews were fair and constructive, and often full of insight. But they were also measured: we get a fuller idea of her real opinions and her sparklingly witty personality in her letters and journals, where she could be completely open and frank. For example, in her journal she mischievously commented on E.M. Forster's novel *Howard's End*: '... it's not good enough. E.M. Forster never gets any further than warming the teapot. He's a rare fine hand at that. Feel this teapot. Is it not beautifully warm? Yes, but there ain't going to be no tea.'

As well as her review column and occasional poetry, Katherine also corrected her friend Koteliansky's translation of the Diary and Letters of Anton Chekhov, both of which were published in the *Athenaeum*, and later contributed several of her own short stories.

Katherine, Murry and his brother Richard at Portland Villas, Hampstead.

Katherine and Ida spent the early part of the winter of 1919 at Ospedaletti on the Italian Riviera. This was the blackest period of Katherine Mansfield's life. She knew she was dying and she was desperately frightened. She felt insecure and believed her husband did not love her – at one stage she even accused him of already thinking her dead. She wrote that Ida, on whom she had to depend absolutely in all practical matters but who was no intellectual companion, was a 'born *Layer Out'* – an undertaker preparing her for death. She was subject to bleak fits of depression and weeping, and she was unable to work. On her good days, she managed to write her book reviews and would post off a full, descriptive letter to Murry. On a bad day she could do nothing. In December she wrote in her journal:

All these two years I have been obsessed by the fear of death. This grew and grew and grew *gigantic*, and this it was that made me cling so, I think. Ten days ago it went. I care no more. It leaves me perfectly cold . . . I am a dead woman and I *don't care*.

Opposite
Promenading along the front in Cannes, 1919.

Murry and Mansfield in Menton on the French Riviera, 1921.

Murry came out for two weeks at Christmas but once again failed to offer Katherine the support and love she needed. Her journal entries of January 1920 read as a morbid catalogue of despair. Perhaps to reproach Murry for his insensitivity in her time of need Katherine sent him 'The Man without a Temperament', a story about a caring husband devoted to looking after his invalid wife, but which dwells on the empty, joyless life they share because of her ill health.

At the end of the month Katherine moved to Menton to stay with her father's elderly cousin, Miss Connie Beauchamp. There, in the luxurious surroundings of the Villa Flora, her depression lifted and by spring she was ready once again to return to England.

Spring and summer passed uneventfully in the 'Elephant', and in September, Katherine and Ida Baker once more set off to spend winter in Menton, this year in the comfortable Villa Isola Bella. This period was an intensely productive one for Katherine Mansfield, and she wrote eight stories in quick succession including the macabre 'Poison', 'Miss Brill', 'The Life of Ma Parker' and, most notably, 'The Daughters of the Late Colonel'. Most of

'This little place is and always will be for me,' wrote Katherine of the Villa Isola Bella, in the south of France.

that you did not live in the time that Motoua did –

Kathleen

K

Kathleen M Beauchamp.

Kathleen Beauchamp.

K. M. Beauchamp.

K. M. Beauchamp.

K. M. Beauchamp.

the best

K. M. Beauchamp.

the stories return to the old Mansfield theme of women suffering alone, often at the mercy of thoughtless men – husbands, fathers or employers – or of cruel circumstance. Both 'Poison' and 'The Stranger' deal with isolation in marriage, and death is central in 'The Life of Ma Parker' and 'The Daughters of the Late Colonel', one of her best works.

'The Daughters of the Late Colonel' tells of two elderly and timid spinster sisters, Constantia and Josephine, after the death of their cruel, domineering father. Years of

Teenage signature practice in a notebook of 1904.

terrified subjugation to his every bad-tempered whim has left them painfully ill-equipped to lead their own lives or to fulfil their own tentative dreams. They fear scorn and derision at every turn, even from their maidservant, Kate. With their father's death they are given their first opportunity to 'turn to the sun' and free themselves to live as *they* want, but sadly the force of habit proves too strong – even after his death these timid creatures cannot escape the clutches of their father's domination:

> Josephine had had a moment of absolute terror at the cemetery, while the coffin was lowered, to think that she and Constantia had done this thing without asking his permission. What would father say when he found out? For he was bound to find out sooner or later. He always did. 'Buried. You two girls had me *buried!*' She heard his stick thumping. Oh, what would they say? What possible excuse could they make?

('The Daughters of the Late Colonel')

As in 'Je ne parle pas français', every word of the story contributes towards our understanding of the central characters, Con and 'Jug'. For example, after a hopeless attempt to clear out their dead father's room:

> They sat down, very shaky, and looked at each other.
> 'I don't feel I can settle to anything,' said Josephine, 'until I've had something. Do you think we could ask Kate for two cups of hot water?'
> 'I really don't see why we shouldn't,' said Constantia carefully. She was quite normal again. 'I won't ring. I'll go to the kitchen door and ask her.'
> 'Yes, do,' said Josephine, sinking down into a chair. 'Tell her, just two cups, Con, nothing else – on a tray.'
> 'She needn't even put the jug on, need she? said Constantia, as though Kate might very well complain if the jug had been there.
> 'Oh no, certainly not! The jug's not at all necessary. She can pour it direct out of the kettle,' cried Josephine, feeling that would be a labour-saving indeed.
> Their cold lips quivered at the greenish brims. Josephine curved her small red hands round the cup; Constantia sat up and blew on the wavy steam, making it flutter from one side to the other.

('The Daughters of the Late Colonel')

Here their timid attitude to their servant, 'proud, young Kate, the enchanted princess'; the way their cold lips 'quiver' nervously; the way they hold their cups; all is balanced to bring, in Katherine Mansfield's own words, 'the deepest truth out of the idea'. The treatment of the story is also in parts extremely humorous though it never, as some contemporary readers thought, mocks the plight of the two vulnerable old ladies.

In December 1920 *Bliss and Other Stories*, a collection of fourteen stories including 'Prelude', 'Je ne parle pas français,','Bliss', 'The Man without a Temperament' and 'Sun and Moon' was published. Katherine Mansfield herself was highly critical of many of the stories in *Bliss*, saying: ' a great part of my . . . book is *trivial*. It's not good enough. You see it's too late to beat about the bush any longer. They are cutting down the cherry trees; the orchard is sold – that is really the atmosphere I want.'

Katherine looking tired and ill as tuberculosis took its hold. She is shown here with Dorothy Brett in 1921.

In fact, the book was well-received, both in England and the USA. Desmond MacCarthy wrote an extremely complimentary review in the *New Statesman* which compared Katherine Mansfield to Chekhov, and other critics mentioned her 'infinitely inquisitive sensibility', the 'shimmering' world she creates.

At the end of 1920 she was no better physically; she had a tubercular gland in her neck which had to be lanced regularly, and she could hardly walk. Her life was that of the invalid: 'I get up about 11. Go downstairs until 2. Come up and lie on my bed until 5 when I get back into it again.' She had learned, too, of Murry's flirtations in London –

one with her painter friend Dorothy Brett, the other with Princess Elizabeth Bibesco – and was angry and hurt by his behaviour. In proud defiance she wrote to Murry:

I have of you what I want – a relationship which is unique but it is not what the world understands by marriage. That is to say I do not in any way depend on you, neither can you shake me ... I am a writer first.

Murry was important, but she now considered that the central purpose of her life was writing. 'More even than talking or laughing or being happy, I want to write.'

6
The Final Stories

Murry came out to Menton for Christmas 1920 to find Katherine seriously ill. The *Athenaeum* was failing, so he decided to give up the editorship and live in the Villa Isola Bella with Katherine and Ida Baker (whom Katherine called her 'wife' and upon whom she now depended in all household and practical affairs). They spent a peaceful few months there until May 1921 then, advised to leave because the Riviera's summer climate was considered too enervating for Katherine's lungs, she and Ida set off for the pure mountain air of Switzerland. After consulting a

'The cleanliness of Switzerland! Darling it is frightening . . . Every daisy in the grass below has a starched frill – the very bird droppings are dazzling,' wrote Katherine of her health retreat in the Swiss Alps.

'I do *lament that he is not warm, ardent, full of quick response, careless, spendthrift of himself, vividly alive — high spirited,'* said Katherine of Murry. *'But it makes no difference to my love.'*

'The Mercury is bringing out that very long seaweedy story of mine 'At the Bay',' wrote Katherine to Dorothy Brett in 1921. 'I feel inclined to suggest to them to give away a spade an' bucket with each copy.'

leading tuberculosis specialist, who would only tell Katherine that she still had a chance of recovery provided her digestion remained robust, they found a villa high up in the mountains at Montana-sur-Sierre. Katherine and Murry spent the next eight months there in easy companionship, enjoying the spectacular mountain scenery, occasionally visiting Katherine's cousin Elizabeth (author of *Elizabeth in her German Garden*) who had a chalet at nearby Randogne, reading the 'old masters' – Chaucer, Shakespeare, Proust and Tolstoy – and, most important of all, working.

In the months from July to October she wrote in intense, feverish bursts, producing much of the fine work for which she is today remembered. 'At the Bay', 'The Garden Party', 'The Doll's House' and 'The Voyage' were all written during this, her final sustained period of creative activity. Perhaps because she knew the time she had left was short, Katherine Mansfield concentrated on disciplining herself to perfect her craftsmanship. Her letters and journal of this time are full of self-criticism: of the need to write more, to write better, to concentrate harder. As a writer she had created an impressionistic form by which she could get the 'deepest truth out of an idea'. Everything had to combine to bring out the completeness of a character or idea, and to be completely true to that character or idea. She often described her method in terms of music or painting. Talking about her story 'Miss Brill', she explained:

> I choose not only the length of every sentence, but even the sound of every sentence. I choose the rise and fall of every paragraph to fit her, and to fit her on that day at that very moment. After I'd written it I read it aloud – numbers of times – just as one would *play over* a musical composition – trying to get it nearer and nearer to the expression of Miss Brill . . . If a thing has really come off it seems to me there mustn't be one word out of place, or one word that could be taken out. That's how I AIM at writing.

(Letter to Richard Murry, 1921)

'At the Bay' is one of Katherine Mansfield's finest pieces of work and is a perfect illustration of her method. In twelve loosely linked episodic passages it follows the course of a single summer day in the life of the extended

Burnell family, already known to us from 'Prelude'. The story is remarkable as a truthful portrayal of general human activity – the pulse, flow and rhythm of life – and as a perfect creation of atmosphere – that of a hot, lazy, seaside day. Katherine Mansfield hoped the story was:

'I hope it is good. It is as good as I can do, and all my heart and soul is in it,' wrote Katherine of 'At the Bay'.

. . . full of sand and seaweed, bathing dresses hanging over verandas, and sandshoes on window sills, and little pink 'sea' convolvulus, and rather gritty sandwiches and the tide coming in. And it smells (oh, I *do* hope it smells) a little bit fishy.

Opposite *A day out at the beach, 1920.*

The story opens simply with the words 'Very early morning' and immediately the curtain rises on a scene of hazy morning mist, of the first faint rays of sunrise, and the expectant awakening of the day to come. The first section is a fluid, evocative piece of descriptive prose and sparkles with Katherine Mansfield's delight in the wonders of nature:

Ah-Aah! sounded the sleepy sea. And from the bush there came the sound of little streams flowing, quickly, lightly, slipping between the smooth stones, gushing into ferny basins and out again; and there was the splashing of big drops on large leaves, and something else – what was it? – a faint stirring and shaking, the snapping of a twig and then such silence that it seemed someone was listening.

('At the Bay', I)

Below *'It was strange that even the sea seemed to sound differently when all those leaping, laughing figures ran into the waves.' ('At the Bay')*

A shepherd passes with his flock of sheep on their way to pasture. Then, rudely breaking the silence of early morning, we are introduced to the faintly ridiculous figure of Stanley Burnell in a 'broad-striped bathing suit', charging down to the beach for his early-morning dip. Here the traditionally masculine figure of Stanley, full of

self-important bluster, is contrasted with that of his sensitive, articulate but ultimately 'weedy' (as Linda later decides) brother-in-law Jonathan Trout.

Then, breakfast. One of Katherine Mansfield's most remarkable gifts was her ability to portray children realistically – the way they talk and think, the games they play, their private world away from the adults. At the breakfast table, we meet Kezia, Lottie and Isabel, and although there is no formal description of them, after just a few sentences we know exactly what each is like and what their relationship is to each other in terms of age and temperament:

> 'Oh Kezia! Why are you such a messy child!' cried Beryl despairingly.
>
> 'Me, Aunt Beryl?' Kezia stared at her. What had she done now? She had only dug a river down the middle of her porridge, filled it, and was eating the banks away. But she did that every single morning, and no one had said a word up till now.
>
> 'Why can't you eat your food properly like Isabel and Lottie?' How unfair grown-ups are!
>
> 'But Lottie always makes a floating island, don't you, Lottie?'
>
> 'I don't,' said Isabel smartly. 'I just sprinkle mine with sugar and put on the milk and finish it. Only babies play with their food.'
>
> (At the Bay, III)

Kezia has a less central role in 'At the Bay' than in 'Prelude', but she is still the creative, 'artistic' child who is fumbling her way towards building her own vision of life.

Amid the deceptively gentle ebb and flow of the Burnell family's day, 'At the Bay' addresses itself to the larger questions of life – of love, marriage and death. The theme of mortality runs consistently through the story, either as the characters themselves reflect on death or the passing of time, or from Katherine Mansfield's constant use of death-related metaphor. Almost the first image we have of the racy Mrs Harry Kember is lying in rigor mortis 'cold, bloody, and still with a cigarette stuck in the corner of her mouth', while Mrs Stubbs talks with gruesome relish about her late husband's ('a burly man with a dead white rose in the button-hole of his coat') demise from dropsy. Death is part of life, and that is most obviously stated in the siesta scene between Kezia and her grandmother:

Red. Nov. 11. 1920

... le your journey ...

My own love ... while I think of it: would it worry you very much to bring your big suit case (registered) with clothes in it ? Things to wear.

'Does everybody have to die?' asked Kezia.
  'Everybody!'
  'Me?' Kezia sounded fearfully incredulous.
  'Some day, my darling.'
  'But, grandma.' Kezia waved her left leg and waggled the toes. They felt sandy. 'What if I just won't?'
  The old woman sighed again and drew a long thread from the ball.
  'We're not asked, Kezia,' she said sadly. 'It happens to all of us sooner or later.'

('At the Bay', VII)

Sketch of the Villa Isola Bella from a letter of November 1920.

The preoccupation with death and its effects on the living are not surprising given Katherine Mansfield's own state of health at the time. Her reflections on love, marriage and the seeming impossibility of true communication between human beings may also be rooted in her own experience. Linda Burnell is the central figure here. She loves her

husband, at least she loves the timid, sensitive, innocent Stanley she is sometimes allowed to see behind the bustling, everyday one:

> But the trouble was . . . she saw *her* Stanley so seldom. There were glimpses, moments, breathing spaces of calm, but all the rest of the time it was like living in a house that couldn't be cured of the habit of catching on fire, on a ship that got wrecked every day. And it was always Stanley who was in the thick of the danger. Her whole time was spent in rescuing him, and restoring him, and calming him down, and listening to his story. And what was left of her time was spent in the dread of having children.

('At the Bay', VI)

Linda was 'broken, made weak' through child-bearing and because of that her feelings for her husband and children are deeply ambivalent. In the poignant scene which follows she surprises even herself when she at last – after the birth of four children – experiences the awakening of the maternal love she thought herself incapable of.

Stanley and Jonathan Trout are two sides of the masculine coin and Linda understands them both. In the garden, she and Jonathan have a sublime, intense moment of true communication. In everyday life, we all experience odd, occasional flashes in which we seem to understand a situation precisely. Katherine Mansfield had the ability to capture the essence of such a fleeting moment: to give a 'swift, illuminated glimpse into a character or situation at a given moment' as one critic put it. It is perhaps this quality which gives her best work the feeling of being so vividly true to life.

In 'At the Bay' as in 'Prelude', Katherine Mansfield was drawing upon her experiences of childhood and family life in New Zealand. Just after finishing the story she wrote. 'I hope it is good. It is as good as I can do, and all my heart and soul is in it . . . every single bit . . . It's so strange to bring the dead to life again . . . I have tried to make it as familiar to "you" as it is to me . . . ' The story ends as it starts, with the cycle of the day: night falls and 'All was still.'

The complex, multi-personal viewpoint of 'At the Bay' contrasts with that of 'The Voyage', written during the

Opposite *Katherine at the Villa Isola Bella: 'My life is the same, I get up at about 11. Go downstairs until 2. Come up and lie on my bed until 5 when I get back into it again.'*

same period. 'The Voyage' is told from the viewpoint of Fenella, a young girl travelling on an overnight boat trip with her grandmother. The story unfolds quietly and unemotionally, and it is with sudden, poignant shock that we realize Fenella's mother has recently died. The childlike choice of metaphor and the characteristically childish flights of fancy – the boat 'beaded with round gold lights . . . looked as if she was more ready to sail among stars than out into the cold sea' – give a perfect insight into Fenella's consciousness and illustrate Katherine Mansfield's ability to get deep into the soul of her characters. In fact, so absorbed did she become in the characters in the story that she jokingly exclaimed: 'I might have remained the grandma for ever after if the wind had changed that moment. And that would have been a little embarrassing for Middleton Murry.'

'The Garden Party' and 'The Doll's House' are also set in New Zealand and both deal with petty social snobbery and class consciousness. In 'The Garden Party', excited, last-minute preparations are being made by the rich, middle-class Sheridan family (recognizably the Burnells, though the children are older) for their party. The story centres on the emotions of Laura who, like Kezia, is artistic,

ffe in a green turban with a dark, wet curl stamped on each of one, the butterfly, always came down on her silk petticoat and kimono collar.

You'll have to go, Laura. You're the artistic one."

way Laura flew, still holding her piece of bread and butter. It's so delicious to have an excuse for eating one of doors. And besides, she loved having to arrange things. She always felt she could do it so much better than anybody else...

Four men in their shirt sleeves, stood grouped together on the garden path.

. Finished and sent to put into my book.

B
This is a wonderfully picturesque thing – and that's all. It's somehow on the episode at the law, stamped –

to go to Sierre if it goes on like this ... or to ——— or to ————

Ka

2

77

Memories of New Zealand inspired much of Katherine's later work. The house on the hill and these slum cottages near Tinakori Road in Wellington were the setting for 'The Garden Party'.

free-thinking and impulsive. In the whirl of pre-party excitement and anticipation, Laura suddenly learns of the accidental death of a labouring man who lived in a nearby cottage. She wants to cancel the party, but her family persuades her against it. Instead, she charitably takes a basket of leftover food down to the dead man's cottage.

Laura's first contact with death, coming as it does so soon after the euphoria of the party, leaves her confused and tearful, but strangely full of wonder. The trip to the cottage has given her a new perspective on her rich, privileged lifestyle: she feels guilt but at the same time cannot help enjoying its luxury. But the story is more than pure social commentary. Katherine Mansfield explained that 'The Garden Party' deals with :

> The diversity of life and how we try to fit in everything. Death included. That is bewildering to a person of Laura's age. She feels things ought to happen differently. First one and then another. But life isn't like that. We haven't the ordering of it.

Laura comes to recognize the helplessness and equality of all humankind in the face of death, but as yet she cannot assimilate her experience into a picture of life as a whole. When discussing the visit with her brother she is too confused to express her feelings coherently: '"Isn't life," she stammered, "isn't life – " But what life was she couldn't explain. No matter. He quite understood.' And the reader is left similarly confused, unsure – as in real life – of the true significance in the random order of events.

Chesney Wold, Karori. 'The house. It was long and low built, with a pillared veranda and balcony all the way round. The soft white bulk of it lay stretched upon the green garden like a sleeping beast.' ('Prelude')

Katherine Mansfield thought 'The Garden Party' only a 'moderately successful story', believing it somehow flawed in the ending passages in the lane. 'The Doll's House', on the other hand, was considered by the novelist J.B. Priestley to be 'a little gem'. It is a well-crafted and realistic story of childhood, and has remained one of Katherine Mansfield's most enduringly popular tales about the Burnell family. Kezia is once again the rebellious central figure. She, Isabel and Lottie are given a 'perfect, perfect' little doll's house which all the girls in their class are invited to see except the Kelveys, the daughters of 'a washerwoman and a jailbird' who were 'shunned by everybody'. Kezia, however, in an act of impromptu generosity, invites the Kelveys into the yard to have a look at the doll's house, where they get told off by Kezia's Aunt Beryl and run away.

Once again the plot is a slight one, and the story is so successful because with perfect economy of language it recreates the world of childhood with all its petty cruelties and copycat adult prejudices. The doll's house itself is a toy of wonder for the children, and is vividly described in the language of children:

> There stood the doll's house, a dark, oily, spinach green, picked out with bright yellow. Its two solid little chimneys, glued on to the roof, were painted red and white, and the door, gleaming with yellow varnish, was like a little slab of toffee. Four windows, real windows, were divided into panes by a broad streak of green. There was actually a tiny porch, too, painted yellow, with big lumps of congealed paint hanging along the edge.

The dialogue, too, is realistically childlike, especially in the scene in the playground when the older girls spitefully torment the Kelveys:

> 'Lil Kelvey's going to be a servant when she grows up.'
> 'O-oh, how awful!' said Isabel Burnell, and she made eyes at Emmie.
> Emmie swallowed in a very meaning way and nodded to Isabel as she'd seen her mother do on those occasions.
> 'It's true – it's true – it's true,' she said.
> Then Lena Logan's little eyes snapped. 'Shall I ask her?' she whispered.
> 'Bet you don't,' said Jessie May.
> 'Pooh, I'm not frightened,' said Lena.

> ('The Doll's House')

In the same scene the girls expose the snobbish attitudes they have already picked up from the adults; even the teacher had a 'special smile for the other children when Lil Kelvey came up to her desk with a dreadfully common-looking bunch of flowers'. Kezia is confused by the arbitrary and unfair rules of the adults and does not understand why the Kelveys are not allowed to come and look at the doll's house. She herself is especially fascinated by the tiny oil lamp inside (a lamp is the traditional symbol of light and knowledge); and her fascination is shared by the sad little figure of Else Kelvey, a 'tiny wishbone of a child' who never smiled and scarcely ever spoke. The story ends on a note of true pathos:

Presently our Else nudged up close to her sister. But now she had forgotten the cross lady. She put out a finger and stroked her sister's quill; she smiled her rare smile.

'I seen the little lamp,' she said softly.

Then both were silent once more.

('The Doll's House')

'There stood the doll's house, a dark, oily, spinach green, picked out with bright yellow. Its two solid little chimneys, glued on to the roof, were painted red and white, and the door, gleaming with yellow varnish, was like a little slab of toffee.' ('The Doll's House')

As with all of Katherine Mansfield's stories of this period, 'The Doll's House' is told in calm, unemotional language. It ranks among her finest work, perhaps because it expresses her most deeply felt belief that: 'Beauty triumphs over ugliness in Life. That's what I feel. And that marvellous triumph is what I long to express.' When the Kelveys see the doll's house and experience that one single moment of beauty, it somehow compensates for the cruel unfairness of their everyday existence. There is more hope for Kezia and these two poor outcasts than for the fierce little adults the other children have become.

7 Searching for a Miracle

The feverish burst of writing in Switzerland left Katherine Mansfield's health worse than ever; she was weak, exhausted and could hardly walk, her teeth were decaying badly and she was in constant pain from rheumatism and her aching lungs. 'One must have a miracle' she wrote and decided in desperation to get in touch with Dr Manoukhin, a Russian exile living in Paris who claimed to be able to cure advanced cases of tuberculosis by bombarding the spleen with X-rays. Murry was totally against the idea: the treatment sounded like expensive quackery (which it was: in the days before antibiotics, the best treatment for TB was complete rest and a good, healthy diet) and even Katherine had some reservations. 'I have the feeling that M[anoukhin] is really a good man,' she wrote. 'I also have a sneaking feeling . . . that he is a kind of unscrupulous imposter.' However, willing to chance anything on the possibility of success, she decided to try his miracle cure. 'After five doses of X-rays one is hotted up inside like a furnace and one's very bones seem to be melting . . . ' she wrote with some humour, given the circumstances. 'If I were a proper martyr I should begin to have that awful smile that martyrs in the flames put on when they begin to sizzle!'

While undergoing the treatment in Paris she wrote a 'queer' and deeply symbolic story called 'The Fly'. A businessman (the 'Boss') is self-consciously grieving for his son, who died in the war six years earlier, when he suddenly catches sight of a fly struggling to get out of the

Opposite *Neither Manoukhin's treatment nor modern medicine could cure Katherine's tuberculosis.*

inkpot on his desk. The man lifts the fly on to his blotting paper, watches it clean itself up ready to fly off again, then sadistically plops a heavy blot of ink down on top of it:

> What would it make of that? What indeed! The little beggar seemed absolutely cowed, stunned, and afraid to move because of what would happen next. But then, as if painfully, it dragged itself forward. The front legs waved, caught hold, and, more slowly this time, the task began from the beginning.
>
> ('The Fly')

The cruel process is repeated until the fly is too exhausted to move and simply dies.

In the story, the fly is the symbol of human life. Katherine Mansfield often used the insect world as a source of imagery in both her letters and stories: in 1918, for example, she wrote to Murry after a harrowing journey to Bandol that: 'I feel like a fly who had been dropped into the milk jug and fished out again, but is still too milky and drowned to start cleaning up yet.' As the fly in the story, 'cowed and stunned', is forced to struggle for life against the thoughtless cruelty of the – at that moment – all-powerful Boss, so do human beings have to struggle against the malicious circumstances of fate. Set in a larger framework, the Boss can also be seen as a victim – he lost his only son during the war – which makes the immense satisfaction he derives from victimizing one weaker than himself even more disturbing.

The tone of the piece is calm but intense, unleavened by humour or by the descriptive passages at which Katherine Mansfield excelled. The character of the Boss, whose sense of true human feeling has completely disappeared since the death of his son, is grotesque yet somehow convincing.

Of all Katherine Mansfield's work 'The Fly' has attracted the most critical attention, perhaps because it presents such a vivid, stark, almost nightmare picture of the earthly scheme of things. Yet her message is so pessimistic that the story cannot properly be considered representative of her work. 'The Fly' is perhaps best seen in context: written when Katherine was undergoing painful treatment in a last-ditch attempt to cure a disease which, in her heart of hearts, she must have known was hopelessly advanced. It is little wonder that at this time her vision of life was a bleak one.

Opposite *'I have never loved you so,' wrote the dying Katherine to Middleton Murry in 1921. 'No, my precious, until now I did not know what it was to love* like this.'

ii
i
1921.

My precious darling,

I shall never forget your
beautiful gesture in handing me that
letter. I read it and I drove home
with you and you are still here. You
have been in every moment of the day;
it is as though you had gone up to
the mountains for a long afternoon.
I have never loved you so. No, my
precious, until now I did not know
what it was to love like _this_. This
peace and this wonderful certainty are
quite new.

Take care of yourself.

*Paris in the late
1920s. 'Ever since I
came to Paris I have
been as ill as ever.'
(Journal)*

In February 1922 Katherine Mansfield's third book, *The Garden Party and Other Stories*, was published to overwhelming critical acclaim. It quickly sold out, then went into second and third editions. The collection included much of the fine work she had written in the autumn of 1921, including 'At the Bay', 'The Garden Party' and 'The Voyage', as well as 'The Daughters of the Late Colonel' and many lesser works. Critics called her 'one of our most notable writers' and praised the book's 'tenderness in its irony, dignity in its tragicomedy'. Katherine Mansfield herself was less ecstatic: on reading the proofs, she commented 'one must risk being seen not at one's best. It's no good hiding the unfavourable photographs though pride wants to'. But despite her own harsh criticism, *The Garden Party* established her reputation as one of the most exciting writers of the age.

After the first stage of Manoukhin's treatment was complete, the Murrys left Paris and returned to Switzerland. Katherine's health was no better and once again Murry seemed unable to offer the support she so desperately needed. Instead, she turned again to the practical, motherly Ida Baker whose uncritical love and devotion, unlike that of Murry, knew no bounds. 'I am almost as ill as ever I was, in every way,' she wrote to Ida. 'I want you if you can come to me . . . [Murry] can never realise what I have to do. He helps me all he can but he can't help me really and the result is I spend all my energy – every bit – in keeping going. I have none left for work . . . ' When Ida arrived, Murry went off to stay at Randogne from where he visited Katherine at weekends, later commenting that he and Katherine had a 'depressing effect' upon one another.

In Switzerland Katherine wrote her will and also a letter to Murry outlining in rather vague terms how she wanted him to dispose of her unpublished work and letters after her death. To understand the outcry that arose in some

Katherine, photographed by Ida Baker, her long-standing friend, who looked after her in Switzerland.

circles when Murry started publishing Katherine's work – from unfinished manuscripts to private letters and journals – it is helpful to look in some detail at both sources. In her will, Katherine stated:

> All manuscripts note books papers letters I leave to John M. Murry likewise I should like him to publish as little as possible and to tear up and burn as much as possible. He will understand that I desire to leave as few traces of my camping ground as possible.

In a loving farewell letter to Murry which she deposited with her bank to be sent only after her death, she wrote:

> All my manuscripts I leave entirely to you to do what you like with. Go through them one day, dear love, and destroy all you do not use. Please destroy all letters you do not wish to keep and all papers. You know my love of tidiness. Have a clean sweep, Bogey, and leave all fair – will you?

There is certainly some ambiguity about the way her wishes are phrased in these two documents, but one fact shines clear – that Katherine Mansfield would have liked her 'camping ground' to be as little exposed to the public eye as possible. However, it is worth noting, as her biographer Claire Tomalin points out, that if she had been set upon it, Katherine could easily have destroyed her journals and unfinished work herself.

As she lost faith and realized that Manoukhin's cure was more a mirage than a miracle, Katherine began to seek other avenues of salvation. She had heard of the teachings of the Greek Armenian George Gurdjieff, who believed that civilization had thrown people out of harmony with themselves, and that to live in true harmony one needed to balance one's intellectual, physical and emotional 'centres'. In practical terms, this meant following a tough regime imposed personally by Gurdjieff, which involved hard but varied physical labour, exercises including dancing, and meditation.

When Katherine, Murry and Ida returned for a brief visit to London in August 1922 (during which Katherine met her father and many of her old friends for the last time) she attended lectures given by Ouspensky, a disciple of Gurdjieff. Inspired, perhaps, by these and by the

Opposite *The mystic George Gurdjieff (1872–1949). Katherine spent her last days at his Insititute for the Harmonious Development of Man in Fontainebleau outside Paris.*

enthusiasm of her old friend and editor A.R. Orage, Katherine took the decision to enter the Gurdjieff Institute for the Harmonious Development of Man at Fontainebleau-Avon, just outside Paris.

It is certain that Katherine Mansfield realized death was near; the X-ray treatment, her last real hope, had failed and she was plunged into a deep spiritual crisis. For true contentment she believed she needed to reject her old, false life – 'I have to die to so much; I have to make such *big* changes' she explained to Murry – and start again.

On her birthday, 14 October, she wrote a poignant definition of her idea of a healthy, fulfilled life:

> By health I mean the power to live a full, adult, living, breathing life in close contact with what I love ... I want to enter into it, to be part of it, to live in it, to learn from it, to lose all that is superficial and acquired in me and to become a conscious, direct human being ... That is what I must try for.

She entered the Gurdjieff Institute in October, and despite complaining of the bitter cold, found happiness and peace in the three months she spent in the lively community. She had written little over the past year, but it seems clear that she wanted to set off in a new literary direction. 'I am at the end of my source for the time being,' she wrote to Murry. 'Life has brought me no FLOW. I want to write – but differently – far more steadily.' Just a week before she died, Katherine explained to her cousin Elizabeth: 'I haven't written a word since October and I don't mean to until the spring. I want much more material; I am tired of my little stories like birds bred in cages.'

But it was too late. Murry, summoned by Katherine by letter, arrived at Fontainebleau on 9 January 1923 to find her 'very pale, but radiant'. That evening as she was going to her room, Katherine started coughing and suddenly 'a great gush of blood poured from her mouth'. Within minutes she was dead.

Opposite *Katherine towards the end of her life: 'My spirit is nearly dead. My spring of life is so starved that it's just not dry.'*

She was buried in the communal graveyard at Avon. As epitaph Murry chose the lines from Shakespeare's play *Henry IV* which Katherine had always loved and had used as the preface to her second book, *Bliss* –

' ... but I tell you, my lord fool, out of this nettle, danger, we pluck this flower, safety'.

8 After Words

'Now the only thing that matters to me is that she should have her rightful place as the most wonderful writer and most beautiful spirit of our time,' wrote Murry after Katherine's death, and so he began a campaign praising and promoting her work, idolizing her as a romantic Keatsian figure who battled heroically against illness, her only weapons her artistic genius and her deep, abiding love for him. It is, of course, a totally false picture, and one which ultimately did no good to the reputations of either Katherine or Murry. (Aldous Huxley, for example, satirized the Murry/Mansfield relationship in the portrayal of Burlap and his dead wife in *Point Counter Point*.) One acerbic critic spoke of Murry 'boiling Katherine's bones to make soup'. D.H. Lawrence chided him for publishing her 'wastepaper basket' and the picture of a saintly, suffering, too-good-for-this-world Katherine which emerged from her carefully edited letters and journal was far from the tough, flamboyant reality. Katherine herself was always deeply suspicious of Murry's tendency to overpraise: 'I don't want dismissing as a masterpiece' she once rebuked him sharply.

In June 1923, *The Doves' Nest and Other Stories* was published. The collection contains a few finished stories – 'The Fly', 'The Doll's House', 'A Cup of Tea', 'The Canary', 'The Honeymoon' – but consists mostly of unfinished fragments written during the last two years of Katherine's life. Then the *Poems* came out (Katherine Mansfield's poetic attempts are slight and are not generally considered

Opposite *Writer and satirist Aldous Huxley, who caricatured the Murrys in his novel* Point Counter Point.

Aldous Huxley.

'I have of you what I want – a relationship which is unique but it is not what the world understands by marriage,' Katherine said of her union with Middleton Murry.

to compare with her short stories), followed in 1924 by *Something Childish and Other Stories*, the fifth and final collection of short stories. *Something Childish* consists of work written mostly during the period 1910 to 1920 but previously uncollected, including 'The Woman at the Store', 'Poison', the sentimental 'Something Childish But Very Natural' and 'An Indiscreet Journey', a rather oblique piece based on Katherine's wartime adventure behind the lines to see Francis Carco.

As well as publishing her stories, Murry also edited and published her *Journal* (1927), *Letters* (1928), (both with all sharp and unflattering comments on friends removed), her book reviews for the *Athenaeum* (in *Novels and Novelists*, 1930), *The Scrapbook of Katherine Mansfield* (1939) culled together from her journals, more letters and a 'definitive' version of the *Journal* (1954). In addition Murry zealously promoted her work in his new magazine, the *Adelphi*.

Murry's motives are difficult to fathom. He took the decision to publish her work – and her obviously private letters and journals – in spite of her will in which she requested him to 'tear up and burn' as many of her 'manuscripts note books papers letters' as possible, and that decision must have weighed heavily upon his conscience. Perhaps Murry truly believed his creation of Katherine Mansfield as suffering genius and therefore found justification in bringing her work – and especially her journal and letters which he considered 'form a single whole with her stories' – to the largest possible audience. (In fairness to Murry it must be pointed out that the letter forwarded to him after her death was much more ambiguous about disposing of her manuscripts than her will. It should also be pointed out that Mansfield's royalties brought Murry financial security for the rest of his life.)

Whatever the morality of Murry's decision to publish, in retrospect we must be thankful to him for preserving the journals and letters, for it is through their pages, rather than through those of her sensitive, 'feminine' stories, that we get a picture of the complex, witty and challenging character of Katherine Mansfield the woman.

Hugh Walpole, a contemporary novelist, considered Katherine Mansfield's talent 'a minor one, but a lovely lasting and enriching one', and perhaps her position in literature's pantheon today confirms that view. But she died prematurely at the age of only 34, and wrote much of her work under the strain of illness and knowledge of impending death. Her major contribution to the history of English literature was in abandoning the conventions of plot, thus bringing a modern tone to the short story. Her genius was in managing by subtle, indirect means to convey the 'over tones, half tones, quarter tones . . . hesitations, doubts, beginnings' of everyday human relationships. Like Jane Austen, her scale was limited and she chose to write about ordinary people living ordinary lives. But she did so vividly and with a sharp eye for nuance and for the observation of human frailty. Her letters and journals show her natural writing ability at its most fluent, a few of her stories show it at its most bold and creative, yet for the most part her talent was greater than her actual achievement. Had she lived a little longer, she might have fulfilled her desire to write a novel, though

The novelist Hugh Walpole (1884–1941) who said of Katherine's talent that it was 'lovely, lasting and enriching'.

the form of the short story was probably her most natural medium because it allowed full range to her outstanding talent for quick, dramatic presentation of scene, excellent dialogue and succinct characterization. As it is, we now value, in the words of the novelist V. S. Pritchett: 'her economy, the boldness of her comic gift, her dramatic changes of the point of interest, her power to dissolve and reassemble a character and situation by a few lines'. In short, the innovative nature of her own, unique literary gift.

Glossary

Ambivalence Opposing feelings of one person towards a single object.

Arbitrary Based on personal whim.

Articulate Able to express oneself fluently.

Avant garde Those writers, artists and musicians who create and support the newest, most experimental ideas.

Bloomsbury group A group of intellectuals, writers and artists including Virginia and Leonard Woolf, Clive and Vanessa Bell, E.M. Forster and Lytton Strachey who lived and worked in Bloomsbury, central London from about 1907 to 1930.

Characterization The creation of fictional characters.

Chronic Constantly recurring.

Controversy Strong disagreement of opinion.

Enervating Weakening.

Epigram Concise, witty saying.

Euphoria A feeling of great elation.

Feminism Belief in equal rights and opportunities for women.

Freudian psychology A method of studying and understanding the human mind.

Hausfrau A German housewife.

Imagery The verbal pictures with which writers convey their meaning.

Impressionism Method of capturing fleeting impressions of reality or of mood, especially used in painting.

Impromptu Spontaneous.

Insipid Lacking interest.

Interior monologue A method of telling a story from the viewpoint of one person by showing the inner workings of his/her mind, often used by the poet Robert Browning and by Katherine Mansfield.

Languid Without energy or spirit.

Metaphor A figure of speech in which an object or person is compared to something else to show a resemblance, e.g. 'he fought like a lion'.

Narrative A story in which events follow on from each other.

Pantheon A show place for all the literary or other figures of the past.

Pathos The power of arousing pity or sorrow.

Personify To represent as a person, to give human characteristics to.

Posthumous After death.

Pseudonym A fictional name adopted by a writer.

Quarterly Occurring four times a year.

Rapacious Extremely greedy.

Reminisce To talk fondly about the past.

Royalty A percentage from the sale of a book given annually to the author by the publisher.

Sardonic Scornful, sneering.

Satire An exaggerated, mocking style that forms a moral commentary on its subject.

Socialism A political and economic theory which states that the means of production and distribution in industrialized societies should be placed in the hands of the whole social community.

Subjugation Living under the strict rule of another.

Succinct Concise.

Suffrage The power of voting.

Supercilious Overbearing in manner, high-handed.

Symbolize Stand for, represent.

Unconventional Free in one's ways, not following the traditional path.

List of Dates

1888	14 October: Kathleen Mansfield Beauchamp born at Tinakori Road, Wellington, New Zealand.
1893	The Beauchamp family move to Karori.
1898	The Beauchamps move back to a large house in Tinakori Road.
1902	Katherine meets the Trowell family.
1903	Katherine and her sisters attend Queen's College, London. Meets Ida Baker.
1906	Returns to Wellington. Grandmother dies.
1907	Katherine goes on trip to outback of North Island. 'In a Café' published in *Native Companion*.
1908	Katherine arrives in London. Falls in love with Garnet Trowell. Becomes pregnant.
1909	Marries and on the same day leaves George Bowden. Miscarries in Bad Wörishofen, Bavaria. Meets Floryan Sobieniowski.
1911	*In a German Pension*. Meets John Middleton Murry.
1912	She and J.M. Murry become lovers. Assistant editor of *Rhythm*.
1913	Meets D.H. Lawrence and Francis Carco.
1915	Visits Francis Carco in wartime France. Brother Leslie Beauchamp killed in France.
1916	Meets Virginia Woolf.
1917	'Spot' found in her left lung. Winters in France.
1918	Marries J.M. Murry. *Prelude* published by Hogarth Press. First tubercular haemorrhage.
1919	Reviewing novels for *Athenaeum*. Spends winter in Italy and France.
1920	*Bliss and Other Stories*. Winters in France.
1921	In Switzerland writing 'At the Bay', 'The Garden Party', 'The Doll's House'.
1922	*The Garden Party and Other Stories*. Undergoing X-ray treatment for tuberculosis. Enters Gurdjieff Institute.

MURRY, JOHN MIDDLETON *Between Two Worlds* (Cape, 1935)

O'SULLIVAN, VINCENT *Katherine Mansfield's New Zealand* (Golden Press, 1974)

TOMALIN, CLAIRE *Katherine Mansfield: A Secret Life* (Viking, 1987; pbk, Penguin, 1988)

Index

Picture acknowledgements

The author and publishers would like to thank the following for allowing their illustrations to be reproduced in this book: the Alexander Turnbull Library, Wellington, New Zealand 9, 10, 11, 12, 13, 14 (by permission of the Mr George Moore Collection, Waikaraka, Masterton), 16, 17, 18, 19, 20, 23, 24, 30, 31, 32, 36, 37, 39, 40, 43, 45, 49, 51, 52, 55, 57, 58, 59, 61, 62, 65, 73, 74, 76, 77, 78, 80, 81, 87, 89, 93, 96; Mary Evans Picture Library 8, 29, 38, 46, 91, 95, 99; the Billie Love Collection 27, 56, 64, 67, 70, 71, 83 (from The Lilliput Antique Doll and Toy Museum, Brading, Isle of Wight), 85; the University of Nottingham 48; Topham Picture Library 7, 22, 26, 35, 44, 54, 68, 88.